X

Judas
the betrayer

Judas
the betrayer

translated from the French

by
Albert Nicole

Baker Book House
Grand Rapids 6, Michigan
nineteen fifty-seven

Judas, The Betrayer

Library of Congress Catalog Card Number: 57-14759
Copyright, 1957, by
Baker Book House

PHOTOLITHOPRINTED BY CUSHING - MALLOY, INC.
ANN ARBOR, MICHIGAN, UNITED STATES OF AMERICA
1957

Contents

Part One

*"Have I not chosen you
twelve, and one of you
is a devil?"* — JOHN 6:70

Part One

Part One

Although the name of Judas with its stigma has become to such an extent the symbol of all treachery and perfidy, and the son of perdition appears to have had such a unique destiny in history, we generally read what the gospel tells us about this melancholy individual without being sufficiently warned by such an example. Certainly, Judas alone, through the force of circumstances, was the one to betray the Son of Man to his enemies, but this treachery does not remain isolated. It is being repeated through all the ages: only the outward manifestation is different.

And we see how cunning the enemy of souls is to deceive those he wishes to lull to sleep; for he not only took possession of Judas during his lifetime, but uses the horror which his crime inspires in us to neutralize the lesson of his life and death. We are apt to forget to notice from point to point the downward path Judas took from his starting point. We are so sure never to reach the same fatal ending.

It is, however, the duty of all the followers of God to warn their brothers, cost what it may. To help us to accomplish this duty, I would like to study with you the character of Judas. I will divide the study into three parts, which we will contemplate in turn. First I will take Judas as the gospel describes him

before the Last Supper. Next we will consider the
tragic struggle which took place at the Last Supper
between Jesus and his rebellious disciple. Finally we
will see the end of the tragedy — Judas after the Last
Supper. This study, I hope, will enable us to examine
our own hearts better, and serve to put us on our
guard against the germs of evil, which are so im-
perceptible at first, but, once having taken root,
become so powerful.

*   *   *

The first time St. John mentions Judas in his
Gospel, he explains these words of Christ, "Have not
I chosen you twelve, and one of you is a devil?" (John
6:70) . What a contrast between the question, "Have
not I chosen you twelve?" and the painful admission
"and one of you is a devil." These words raise ques-
tions of vital importance in our mind. To the practical
solution of these we should like in the first place to
devote some time.

We have often wondered why Christ, who knew
everything and whose vision penetrated the greatest
depths of the most secret places of the heart, should
choose for one of his disciples a man so unnatural as
to betray the Son of Man afterwards, and one day
be disgraced before all by having to bear the terrible
epithet of "devil," which even our versions have not
dared to render with all the strength of the original
text. Was Christ mistaken at the time he made his
choice especially as he had passed the whole night in
prayer? Must we believe that he intentionally chose
a traitor among his twelve so that the Scriptures might
be fulfilled and the mission performed, which he was

meant to accomplish that night, which through all the ages will be called "the night that Jesus was betrayed"? All our moral sense, however, protests against such a supposition.

In reality Judas did not stop his downward course from the moment of his calling till the day Christ says, "One of you is a devil," that is, a being who is in the power of the devil, because he is akin to him. The extraordinary severity of this revelation, and the circumstances which immediately preceded it, as well as the other incidents in the life of Christ that Judas witnessed, and in which he even took an active part, seem to present a collection of contradictory words and facts. And it is just these contradictions which put us on the track of the real interpretation. You must also notice that Jesus does not say "one of you was a devil when I chose you." He became one. One could, therefore, be a disciple and have been chosen by the Saviour from amongst those who crowded around him; one could have been an apostle and have passed months, perhaps even years, in the most intimate society of our Lord; one could have been a witness of his miracles, a listener to all his teachings and as such have been sent to announce the kingdom of heaven, to drive out devils, to heal the sick, to give freely what one had freely received; one could even have been used in the conversion of souls, and all the same become a devil! Thus we will see in studying the character of Judas how this transformation took place in him. And were it not for the circumstances which have given to his crime its unique character, how we might all become Judases! It is, consequently, a psychological

problem of the greatest practical interest and importance.

The gospel explains this problem in two ways, one
of which does not as a rule sufficiently attract our
attention. The epithet which is nearly always attached
to the name Judas or that of his father determines his
native town. *Iscariot* means "the man of Keriot." This
is important because it is not only to tell us the name
of Judas' birthplace and cast a slur on it that the
gospel indicates the origin of the man for whom it
would have been better had he never been born and
never seen the light of day. This information is given
us to explain the reasons which prompted him to offer
his services to Christ.

The town of Kerioth is situated in Judea (Joshua
15:25) in the Roman province. While the other
disciples were, in all probability, Galileans, that is,
subjects of Herod Antipas, Judas was a Judean, that
is a Roman subject. Now while a certain independence
was granted to the Galileans, the inhabitants of Judea
were ruled by a Roman governor. They felt the for-
eign yoke weigh more heavily on their shoulders and,
consequently, awaited the coming of the promised deliverer with more impatience.

Judas may have been in this state of mind when he
heard for the first time the lively word, the persuasive
voice, and the eloquent preaching of Jesus. The Messianic hopes of his fellow countrymen immediately
awoke in him also and, full of enthusiasm, he joined
the other disciples, attracted as he was by the same
hopes. The miracles that Jesus performed left no

doubt but that he was the deliverer their ambitions had pictured; and Judas at the very beginning even more than the other eleven disciples cherished the idea that their Master would re-establish the kingdom of Israel. This prospect enticed him to become one of the disciples of the future king and consequently one of the trustees of his sovereign authority.

The other eleven, without doubt, looked forward to an ending of this preparatory stage which made Christ wander from one city to another, from one village to another without having where to lay his head. They were all upheld by the hope of the glorious time when their beloved Master would reign over Israel and over all nations. However, these were but secondary motives for them as we see from Peter's exclamation, "Lord, to whom shall we go? Thou hast the words of eternal life" (John 6:68). They much more ardently wished to satisfy the longing of their souls than to see the ambition of their people realized. And although they were torn in the beginning between these two desires, their hearts were gradually conquered by the ideal of Christ who thrust aside all political intrigue, and was content to announce the glad tidings and to heal the sick instead of proclaiming himself the expected Messiah.

It is true, even the eleven still had much to learn (Acts 1:6). But they submitted to the influence of their Master, whereas Judas who was from the beginning a more ardent patriot than a believer, always fostered the material element in himself at the expense of the divine. But, if ambition partly inspired the conduct of the others, if dreams of personal glory mingled

with those inspired by their patriotism, there was still
another reason which influenced Judas. It was his love
of money.

We do not think that we are wrong to speak of
this passion in Matthew, the man who was a thief six
days before the passover, according to the Gospel
of St. John (John 12:6). He became a disciple and
then an apostle through interest. While the others
offered, at least in part, their services to Jesus Christ
out of love for him and with a desire to serve him,
Judas had an ulterior motive. He hoped to derive some
financial benefit from his position. This is the second
trait which helps us to unravel the tragedy of which
the soul of Judas was the stage.

Imagine the continual watch which a man in such
surroundings had to impose upon himself! Everything
he loved was despised by his immediate associates.
Everything he despised was revered by them. The
parables of Jesus about the vanity of wealth seemed to
be directly addressed to him. Every time Christ looked
at him he feared that he had been discovered. There
was only one possible way to escape from this situation
— to accept the consequences of the error he had committed and, after having recognized that he had been
mistaken in following the Galilean prophet, to leave
him forever. One day an opportunity had been offered
him. The mob animated by this same spirit seemed
to beckon to him to follow their example. Did he not
realize the intention of Jesus in pronouncing these
words to the twelve, but which were particularly per-
tinent to him, "Will ye also go away?" The crisis
through which he had passed had not yet sufficiently

affected him to unmask his true character. When, therefore, Peter, with his usual impetuosity, answered in the name of all, without knowing whether all agreed with him, "Lord, to whom shall we go? Thou hast the words of eternal life," Judas remained under the hypocritical cloak of this confession, notwithstanding the words of Christ, "Have not I chosen you twelve, and one of you is a devil?" The question of Jesus spoken mercifully, advised the man of Kerioth to rejoin those who were going away before entangling himself in an irreparable crime.

John alone allows us to penetrate the tragedy which then was enacted in the dark and troubled soul of Judas. He, alone, also shows us Judas protesting against the wastefulness of Mary, the sister of Lazarus, who had anointed the feet of Jesus with costly ointment. What a contrast! On one side we see love unable to express itself in words inspiring the symbolical act which, through all ages wherever the gospel is preached, will serve as an example for the faithful followers of Christ. On the other side we see long suppressed hatred suddenly breaking out in violent protestations, which also serves indirectly to show us what an apostle may become if he lets himself be governed by a bad passion instead of conquering it. The love of Mary and the hatred of Judas enabled them to guess what to the others was a mystery, for they knew that the moment was approaching when Christ was going to be crucified. This certainty urged Mary to show deepfelt gratitude to our Lord, and drove Judas to abandon a forlorn cause which could not be served without danger, and which had become loathsome to him, because it demanded everything and gave nothing in the material possessions which he so greatly desired.

We are now at a turning-point in the history of the gospel, and it is not only to give us some historical indication that John opens his account with these words, "Then Jesus, six days before the passover" (John 12:1). It is especially to make us understand that the following events in spite of their slight importance exercised a decisive influence in the tragedy of Calvary and on Judas, one of the principal characters in this tragedy. His enthusiasm of the beginning has turned into real hatred, for he does not want to make a complete sacrifice of self to Jesus. And as he is in the wrong and does not wish to admit it, he adopts the attitude that all take in similar circumstances: he hates the person who wishes to save him from his sad fate, and the more tender the efforts of Christ are, the more acute will the resistance of Judas become. He even reaches the point where he could not bear to see the others show their affection to the person who had become an object of hatred to him.

For several weeks, therefore, Judas has been watching for a favorable opportunity to run away with a larger sum of money than his purse actually contained. Once already he had seen his chance slip away through the fault of the rich young man; and while the Master followed the young man with a sad look as he was going away, Judas' thoughts were running in quite another direction. Those great riches which, according to the word of Christ, should have been given to the poor, that is, entrusted to him, had slipped from his grasp. Thus he, for whom love of money was a dominating passion, who through this passion became a thief and finally betrayed his Master, cursed the young man who went away feeling grieved because he could not renounce the possessions on which Judas was already counting.

A second time his hopes were disappointed when Zacchaeus of Jericho said to Jesus, "Behold, Lord, the half of my goods I give to the poor" (Luke 19:8). But the chief of the toll collectors preferred to attend to the accomplishment of his own without the help of Judas. The half of his goods represented a considerable sum and again he saw great riches escape his grasp.

And now, a third opportunity was not more fruitful than the others. Instead of selling her ointment for three hundred pence, Mary, without any apparent reason, poured it over Jesus' feet. This time he could not contain his anger and burst forth, "To what purpose is this waste? Why was not this ointment sold for three hundred pence and given to the poor?" (Matt. 26:8, John 12:5).

These are the first words of Judas which the gospel has transmitted to us, and they are singularly revealing. They make us recognize with what diabolical cunning he was able to use a religious varnish to hide his true feelings, and give to his selfish interest the appearance of virtue. Nothing, indeed, vexes the avaricious more than the care of the poor, but Judas had sufficiently studied the thoughts of Jesus and his disciples not to betray himself. He even succeeded in leading astray the others, as we know from Matthew and Mark who report their murmurings, while John mentions the culprit and adds these expressive words, "This he said, not that he cared for the poor; but because he was a thief, and had the bag, and bare what was put therein." The apostle ends his story with these words, which, to our knowledge, are the first which Jesus addressed to the man of Kerioth, "Let her alone: against the day of my burying hath she kept this. For the poor always ye have with you; but me ye have not always" (John 12:7,8).

Matthew, who establishes a close connection between the irritation of Judas at the house of Simon the leper and his proceedings with the chief priests, opens his story with a significant word which we generally read without paying much attention to it: "Then," that is, after Jesus' reply to Judas "let her alone." It is this tender reprimand so kindly spoken and full of love which provoked such an outburst of hatred.

But what should the other eleven have done, to whom, according to Matthew and Mark, the reprimand of Christ was also addressed? How should Martha have acted who had even heard more severe words ring in her ears, "Martha, Martha, thou art careful and troubled about many things; but one thing is needful" (Luke 10:41,42). What should Peter have said whom our Lord had reprimanded so often before everybody and particularly at Caesarea Philippi when he said, "Get thee behind me, Satan: thou are an offense unto me; for thou savourest not the things that be of God, but those that be of men" (Matt. 16:23). Why should we be astonished at this difference in the actions of the persons whose history has been told us by the gospel? Do we not know that a reproach provokes either repentance or resentment, according to the feelings of the person to whom it is addressed? Therefore, when Christ turned to Judas and addressed him directly in giving him his simple order, "Let her alone," and asked so tenderly, "Why trouble ye the woman?" in spite of all the kind solicitude with which he treated this proud soul, Judas heard ringing in his ears the echo of the words of Jesus, which he believed were a direct challenge to his ambitious hopes. "Then," we are told, he went in to the chief priests and said unto them "What will ye give me and I will deliver him unto you?" (Matt. 26:14,15). These are the indications which Matthew gives us to explain the motives which dictated Judas' conduct, and he reveals them in this simple word "Then."

But Luke, who does not relate the incident which took place in the house of Simon the leper, reveals the invisible guest taking his abode in the heart of Judas, profiting by the bad feelings he had allowed to foster there and deriving some benefit by his death. Thus, one apostle admirably completes the impression which the other one has given us. One shows the ulterior motives for this sinister proceeding, while the other shows us the inward forces at work acting directly on the will of the traitor until they finish by conquering it entirely. Judas, therefore, when he had closed his heart to Jesus, opened and delivered it to the devil. He who had dared to think that Jesus, Who is Truth, had deceived him, listened to the insinuating voice of the father of all lies. He who had not wished to be revivified by the Prince of life allowed himself to be led astray by a "murderer from the beginning" (John 8:44).

But what were the reasons which inspired Satan with this idea? Luke ends his version of the temptation with these expressive words which I translate literally, "After having tempted him in every way, the devil departed from him until a suitable opportunity" (Luke 4:13). And now, at last, this opportunity had come! The devil's chance had arrived. Chaos and turmoil reigned supreme! The priests had decided to put Christ to death. Caiaphas, the chief priest, declared, "It is expedient for us that one man should die for the people and that the whole nation perish not," but they were afraid of a revolt of the people. These murderers, although they had decided to put him to death, did not know how to accomplish their plans. It was then that Satan put into the heart of Judas the idea to betray his Master.

Jesus should not, Judas thinks, be killed by the dagger of an assassin. This death would be too sudden, and would not allow a display of all the temptations and sufferings with which he desires to overwhelm his victim. Christ should be arrested as an evildoer. He should hear the representative of Jehovah accuse him of blasphemy. He, the Son of God, should witness the outburst of anger against Him by all the members of the Sanhedrin. He should endure insults and be spat upon by the people. He should be condemned to death by the religious authorities of the chosen nation. He should be delivered to Pilate, the Roman governor. He should be witness to the struggle which would take place between Pilate, the representative of pagan justice and the Jews who would imploringly demand his crucifixion. He should have to bear the contempt of Herod and the derision of his courtiers. He, who was love itself, would be an object of hatred because the priests after having accused him of revolt against Caesar would demand of Pilate the release of Barabbas, who was condemned for sedition. In their blindness the Jews would deny their Messiah, crying, "We have no king but Caesar" (John 19:15) and sign the condemnation, "His blood be on us, and on our children" (Matt. 27:25). On the cross He would be exposed to the mockery of the chief priests and scribes and elders, "He saved others; himself he cannot save" (Matt. 27:42).

But the suffering which must have been particularly painful to the Divine Master was the thought of having been betrayed by one of his own, one of those whom he had chosen to announce to the world the glad tidings of the kingdom of God. Yes, one of the twelve would betray him to his enemies. The favourable moment had come now for the devil to attack the Son of Man!

Does it not seem to us that we can hear the insinuating voice of the tempter say to Christ, "Thou hast one day asserted before the Jews: 'My sheep hear my voice, and I know them, and they follow me: And I give unto them eternal life; and they shall never perish, neither shall any man pluck them out of my hand' (John 10:27,28). Thou basest these assertions on the unshakable confidence in God because thou hast added 'My Father which gave them me, is greater than all; and no man is able to pluck them out of my

Father's hand' (John 10:29). Call upon Thy Father
now that he should show his power and keep Judas
from obeying me! 'While I was with them in the world,
I kept them in thy name: those that thou gavest me
I have kept, and none of them is lost, but the son of
perdition, that the scripture might be fulfilled' " (John
17:12). Luke gives us this premonition when he says:
"Then entered Satan into Judas surnamed Iscariot"
The three evangelists, who have related this story to
us, likewise emphasized this fact, reminding us with insistence that Judas was one of the twelve; they would
have us remember the words of Christ during the last
hours before his condemnation so that we might
measure the depth of the anguish which Satan made
Him suffer by this terrible blow.

But that is not the only vision that this account gives
us in its admirable conciseness, for these simple words,
"He went to the chief priests to betray him" (Mark
14:10), make us feel how hateful was such a proceeding. The meeting between the chief priests and
Judas, one of the twelve, was for the purpose of treason,
and it was he who took the first step. In spite of all
their hatred and cynicism the opponents of Christ
would never have dared to go to an apostle to propose
such a bargain. Does it not seem to us that we see
Judas going out of the house of Simon the leper
glancing furtively round him to see if he were not
discovered? But while he was turning over in his mind
this interview with the enemies of his Master, the
road along which he was going reminds him of different incidents of our Lord's journey to Jerusalem.
Some act of strength suddenly comes back to his mind,

and merciful words full of good advice seem to ring in his ears. All this comes back to his mind because he was at a turning point in life when all the past reappears with surprising vividness.

But far from dissuading him from his plan, these visions only strengthened his determination, because he who acted with compassion to strangers, had done nothing to recompense the faithfulness of his disciples. He hastened his step, and having arrived there, asked the chief priests without further preliminaries the question which he had prepared in his mind, "What will ye give me, and I will deliver him unto you?" (Matt. 26:15). These words make us tremble with horror, but they filled the chief priests with joy. They had not counted on receiving such precious help to execute their plan. They concealed their joy, however, because they wanted to obtain their victim at the lowest possible price, and thus commences an odious bargaining. Bargaining! There is no term in any language to express the loathing reprehension one feels to see the chief priests, the representatives of Jehovah on earth, and Judas, one of the apostles and therefore one of the witnesses and intended preachers of the gospel, bargain as to the price Jesus of Nazareth was worth — He whom they should have recognized as the Messiah, and Judas as his Master, and whom the faithful followers, through all times, have recognized as the Saviour of the world and the only Son of God!

Will you say that the gospel does not give us the successive phases of this procedure? That is true, but still Luke expressly tells us that "They were glad and covenanted to give him money; and he promised"

(Luke 22:5,6). What can this mean except that they were not agreed for some time? All this has taken time and Judas wonders if his absence has not been noticed. The chief priests take advantage of this circumstance to give him as little as possible. One is surprised that Judas was content with such a small sum. The first plausible explanation is that the thirty pieces of silver, of which Matthew speaks, were only the first install-ment. He would then have received a promise of more, the crime once having been committed. However, one must remember the special circumstances of the bar-gaining and draw attention to the short time which was at his disposal to discuss matters with the chief priests and persuade them to pay him a price more in proportion to the service rendered them. He re-turns to Bethany in great haste, wondering whether his Master was not going to ask him the same question that of old Elisha asked his servant Gehazi, "Whence comest thou?" But no one appears to have noticed his absence and the story ends with this mournful as-sertion, "And from that time he sought opportunity to betray him." What a conclusion!

And what thoughts these simple words awaken in our mind — "he sought"! The expression is found in three sacred documents, and the verb and the tense which is used give us an impression of extraordinary power. It is in the imperfect, which means that several times during the following days, Judas wondered if the moment had come to betray his Master. And we know what happened during these days, for it is about just these days that we have the most details, and however vaguely they may be present to our mind, we can understand all the tragedy of this search through all the ups and downs of the fierce struggle which the elders of the people waged against Jesus. Pharisees, Herodians, Sadducees, scribes and doctors of the law attacked him furiously. They set traps for him, and tried to confuse him in his speech, but despite their hatred were confounded by the wisdom of his answers. The mob was filled with enthusiasm. The disciples consciously or subconsciously were filled with joy, for it seemed to them that the reign of the Messiah was near. Judas saw and heard all this, but continued his work. In order to betray our Lord to his enemies who were lying in wait for him, he was seeking a suitable opportunity!

Part Two

Part Two

"Then Judas, which betrayed him, answered and said, Master, is it I?" — MATTHEW 26:25

Part Two

We left Judas seeking for a suitable opportunity to betray his Master. Let us, in thought, proceed to the guest chamber. On the way there is strife among the disciples as to which of them should be accounted the greatest. Judas also vies with the others in expounding his arguments, and holding his head high, enters the guest chamber that he may be the first to leave to perpetrate his terrible crime. Christ assigns to each of his disciples the place which has been destined for him. The gospel specially mentions the place that was reserved for the disciple that Jesus loved, and it allows us to guess the one that Judas occupied. To be able to do that we must anticipate a little what we will have to say when we study together the tragic conversation which immediately preceded the second designation of the traitor.

Let us, first of all, take the account which John has given us. Four persons are named. Jesus, Simon Peter, Judas and the disciple that Jesus loved. We are told that John was leaning his head on Jesus' bosom which is explained by the manner in which the guests were seated at table. Who was on His other side? It is evident from the text that it was not Simon Peter, because he would not have beckoned to John that he should "ask who it should be of whom he spake"

(John 13:24). Then who was it? We shudder at pronouncing the name of the man who was honored by our Lord with such a mark of distinction, but the text, as we see it before us, does not allow us to come to any other conclusion. This man was Judas. And if we still have any doubt, I think that the Gospel of St. Matthew will dispel it. All the disciples were exceedingly sorrowful at hearing their Master say that one of them would betray him. And as they had implicit confidence in his word, they asked, "Lord, is it I?" (Matt. 26:22). Judas asked very much the same question as the others, and Jesus answered with these terrible words, "Thou hast said" (Matt. 26:25). Is it plausible to think that the other eleven could have heard Jesus' answer to Judas without doing everything in their power to render it impossible for the traitor to harm their beloved Master? To explain their silence and inaction there is only one possibility, which is, that they did not hear the terrible revelation which Christ made to Judas. And for that to be possible, it was necessary for our Lord to speak in such a way that Judas alone could hear him, which means that Jesus was seated between the disciple he loved and him who was going to betray him. What an appeal to the impenetrable mystery of divine love! But Judas remained unreceptive. He hardened himself, on the contrary, and deduced from this fact a proof of his security for he thought, "If he knew what I am going to do, he would not give me this place."

Now the voice of Jesus made itself heard, but the words which he spoke to all were particularly addressed to Judas. Christ tried to soften his heart: "With desire I have desired to eat this passover with you before I suffer. For I say unto you that I will not any more eat thereof until it be fulfilled in the kingdom of God" (Luke 22:15,16). That was an appeal that should have touched Judas. If the slightest atom of humanity had remained in the heart of this traitor, he would have been touched by the prospect of suffering, foretold with so much calmness. But Judas had hardened his heart too much for any humane feelings to be able to penetrate it. Will he be accessible to arguments in his own interest? And did not the comparison of the kingdom of heaven with a meal bring back to his mind the parables where Christ spoke of the servant who will be cast into outer darkness, and the foolish virgins who find the door shut? These warnings appear to be particularly addressed to Judas, for let us not forget that at the moment they were uttered, Judas had already concluded his odious bargain with the chief priests. Did he not begin to wonder in his mind whether he had perhaps made a mistake? Whether they were really on the eve of unexpected events? From the depths of suffering of which the Master spoke would he suddenly be raised up to glory? Would not that be the hidden and mysterious sense of this prophesy which crowned the somber perspective of the future, "And the third day he will arise from the dead"? What would then happen if, clothed with all the glory of a powerful Messiah, He would come back a second time to punish the rebels? What terrible punishment would then be inflicted on his enemies! What should I have to fear from His anger, I, one

of the twelve, for having betrayed him to the chief
priests and accepted payment for his life blood? Was
the day approaching when, according to his word,
"The Son of man shall send forth his angels, and they
shall gather out of his kingdom all things that offend,
and them which do iniquity"? (Matt. 13:41). And must
I soon hear the judgment, "Depart from me ye cursed,
into everlasting fire, prepared for the devil and his
angels"? (Matt. 25:41).

To the general astonishment, however, our Lord
rises from the table, takes off his clothes, girds himself
with a towel, pours water into a basin and begins to
wash the feet of his disciples and dry them with the
towel with which he was girded. St. John tells us that
Peter protested vehemently against this act of deep
humiliation. He tells us nothing like that about Judas.
And yet if any one of the twelve should have protested
it was surely he! Knowing what he knew, how could
he suffer the man whom he was betraying to humble
himself thus? He sees our Lord coming towards him.
Will he pass him by? What do the mysterious words
mean which were without doubt, addressed to Peter,
"And ye are clean, but not all" (John 13:10). Do
they not make a shudder of horror surge through the
soul of Judas, who knew why Christ was obliged
to make that restriction? Jesus approached, and kneel-
ing down before Judas as he had done before the
others, begins to wash his feet. Although the gospel
remains silent on this point, can you not imagine our
Lord looking at his disciple with unutterable tenderness, "Behold, I stand at the door and knock"
(Rev. 3:20). When did he knock harder or with

more insistence, with more complete self-denial or with a love more divine than when he knelt down to wash the feet of Judas? The traitor notices this look and feels on his body the trembling of the hands which betrays the emotion of him who tries this as a last resort to bring back the lost sheep. Judas observes all that. He remains unmoved. Does he believe it possible to escape the discernment of our Lord, and was he using all his control not to betray himself, he who had betrayed Jesus Christ? Why, then, after having searched the heart of Judas does Christ bend his head lower, and appear to be wholly absorbed in this act of humiliation? Why do his hands tremble as he accomplishes his task? Why does a furtive tear fall on the feet of him who was bringing treacherous tidings? Do you say that John tells us nothing about all this, that he does not even accentuate by a single word this action of Jesus towards Judas? Must the gospel tell us everything? When it sets forth certain facts, does it not, in a way, invite us to complete what it tells us? What a climax! Jesus washing the feet of Judas!

At last Christ has finished his work. He takes the towel with which he was girded and, still in silence, dries the feet which he had washed. Judas feels reassured. Perhaps He did not know! Perhaps He had only some faint suspicion! Perhaps . . . . and it is possible for Judas to entertain this doubt in his soul, because he does not understand how in His merciful tenderness the Lord could content Himself with saying, "And ye are clean, but not all."

But now after having washed the feet of his disciples and taken his garments, Christ seats himself once more

at the table, and addressing the twelve says, "Know
ye what I have done to you?" (John 13:12). Did Judas
understand, or was he hoping that Christ did not know
who was going to betray him because he had humil-
iated himself before him as he did before the others?
Jesus treated him as a disciple, but he used the
privileges of a disciple to seek a suitable opportunity
to betray his Master! What does this puzzling declaration mean: "And ye say well; for so I am" (John
13:13)? One generally translates this part of the
phrase, "And ye say well; for I am he" that is to say,
"I am the Master and the Lord." But the text appears
to me to have quite another meaning. These words
"I am" as Jesus pronounced them refer to the passage
in Exodus where Jehovah speaking to Moses says, "I
am that I am" (Ex. 3:14). What are the answers to
Judas' perplexities? He was wondering if Jesus knew
the name of the traitor, and here Christ affirms his
identity with God Eternal himself, thus most calmly
justifying the titles, "Lord," which his disciples give
him, and "Master," which Judas exclusively calls him.
It is only He who in such an absolute way can say
"I exist" and who alone has consequently neither beginning nor end.

But then what an end is awaiting Judas! These
words which were uttered at such a moment did not
move him. He even sinks deeper and deeper into his
crime. How gradual is his downward course in evil!
Judas by stifling the voice of his conscience allowed
himself more and more to be governed by him who,
according to the tragic expression of John "entered

into him," and finally cause to betray him who is
the source of life, who possesses life in himself — God
manifest in the flesh!

By what false arguments and diabolical suggestions
did Judas reach such conclusions? Does he not retreat
horror-stricken from the path he had chosen? "If he is
Jesus," he said to himself, "nothing should be able to
harm him. How could one kill Life? But if he is not
really the Messiah, I risk nothing. On the contrary,
I shall have delivered my nation from an impostor."
Do not think that I am exaggerating. I am only trying, with the help of Holy Scripture, to follow in the
soul of Judas the successive degrees of his hardening,
not specially with the aim of explaining the psychology
of the traitor, but to render intelligible by this terrible
example what may happen to a man even placed in
the most favourable conditions when he strays from
the straight and narrow way of duty.

Nature does not show us such abnormal phenomena
— the lamb taking the part of the wolf which wishes
to devour it against the shepherd who risks his life
to save it. But alas, in the Kingdom of grace, Judas
is not the only example of such a monstrosity. Thus
continues the sad struggle between our Lord who
wishes to save and the apostle who surrenders himself
more and more to Satan.

"If I then, your Lord and Master, have washed your
feet; ye ought also to wash one another's feet. For I
have given you an example, that ye should do as I
have done to you. Verily, verily, I say unto you, The
servant is not greater than his lord; neither he that

is sent greater than he that sent him. If ye know these things, happy are ye if ye do them" (John 13:14-17). We understand very well the first part of this declaration — the example of humility which he had given to his disciples. But why should they be happy if they knew and practised "those things" which appear to be evident, that is, that the servant is not greater than his Master, nor the apostle greater than him who has sent him? Taken literally this sentence does not appear to us to fit in well with what either precedes or follows it. Why should it be prefaced by these words which contain this solemn declaration, "Verily, verily, I say unto you"? Recall these declarations to your mind, which especially in St. John are thus emphasized by Jesus himself, for they bear upon most vital points of religion and morals.

These words of Jesus, besides those we have been meditating on, appear to make an exception to this rule, but in reality confirm it. They contain Jesus' prediction to Peter that he would deny him (John 13:38) ; and how important was this warning to Simon Peter! For in these words the Resurrected One announced to the same apostle by which death He was going to glorify God. For the first time the Master clearly states the crime of which one of the twelve would be guilty. But for Judas this prophecy was, as we shall see, only one of the warnings which Christ in his mercy gave this last evening to him who was going to betray Him. Thus we cannot answer the question that we asked just now. The statement, "The servant is not greater than his lord; neither he that is sent greater than he that sent him," without apparent connection with the text that either precedes or follows it, was an appeal addressed to Judas — and what an appeal! These words were meant to bring to mind the circumstances which prompted Christ to utter them in the course of instruction that he had given to his apostles whom he sent to announce that the kingdom of heaven was at hand. They were meant to remind Judas of the affirmation which followed them, "If they have called the master of the house Beelzebub, how much more shall they call them of his household?" (Matt. 10:25). Jesus was then speaking to all the disciples, but now he specially turned to Judas to prove that, because he could read the most secret thoughts of his heart, his crime was known to him, and that if he did not reveal the name of the traitor, it was proof of his infinite love which prompted him to give Judas an opportunity of retracing his footsteps without feeling disgraced before everyone. The traitor supposed that he would acquire the goodwill of the priests and scribes through his crime, but Christ dissuaded him. The enemies of yesterday would not be reconciled by this great crime nor would they forget the time when they saw him following Christ, and even though he was a traitor he would always be regarded by them as the servant of Jesus, and consequently treated as such. They received him with joy because he served their purpose. They would thrust him aside with disgust when they had nothing more to expect from his services. And that was the fate that Jesus prophesied for him, and not only that, but these words, "he that is sent" and "he that sent him" make him remember the period

of his life and all the privileges during the journey, at
the beginning of which Jesus had said to him as to
the others also, "Behold, I send you forth" (Matt.
10:16). Briefly, Judas remembered everything that
his duties as well as his privileges implied. He sees himself as he was then, full of zeal and ardor and animated
only by the words which he was instructed to preach
that "the kingdom of God is at hand." He also then
had cast out demons, healed the sick, cleansed the
lepers and raised the dead. And by whom was this
power given him? By the Master whom he was now
going to betray for thirty pieces of silver! Was he not
going to repent and be convinced of his madness?

After this warning which was expressly addressed to
Judas, Jesus says to his disciples, "If ye know these
things, happy are ye if ye do them." And these words
still more specially concern the traitor, as we see from
the limitation which immediately follows, "I speak not
of you all" (John 13:18). Of whom did he speak here?
He referred to him who knew these things perfectly
without putting them into practice. So our Lord, in
contradistinction to this worldly knowledge, adds, "I
know whom I have chosen"; literally, "I know those
that I have chosen" which makes the difference still
more striking between what the disciples knew and
what Christ knew. The traitor in his blindness
imagined, as many others do, that he was sheltered
from all reproach because he knew the truth. This
pretended wisdom, according to the Master, will not
be able to make a man happy who does not conform
his life according to the truth he knows.

Besides, this sentence "I know whom I have chosen"

evokes to Judas' memory the answer to Peter's declaration, "And we believe and are sure that thou art that Christ, the son of the living God." Christ answered, "Have not I chosen you twelve, and one of you is a devil?" (John 6:69,70). Judas was thus reminded of the scene and hears the words which provoked it. He sees in his mind's eye the events of the day and night which preceded them. In thought, he is carried to the top of the mountain in the midst of the multitude which Jesus miraculously feeds with five loaves and two fishes. Again he hears the enthusiasm of the five thousand who cry, "This is of a truth that prophet that should come into the world" (John 6:14). What a wonderful moment! Then everything seemed to favour his ambition! With what enthusiasm he went from group to group of this excited crowd to encourage them to carry off Jesus and make Him their king! It was therefore a great disappointment to him when the Master, instead of letting himself be carried away by this current of strong feeling, fled to escape the crown which they wished to place on his head!

Judas hears again the disciples debating in the boat when Christ commanded them to leave. The wind which was against them forced them to row with all their strength and to think no more of the day's experience. Suddenly, in the night, a human form walking on the waves and struggling against the wind came toward them. Judas still feels surging through his veins the thrill which filled them all with terror. But a well-known voice answered to allay their fears, "It is I, be not afraid" (John 6:20). He sees Peter get out of the boat and go to meet Jesus. Suddenly, Judas, who was following all the movements of Peter, sees him sinking; but our Lord stretched out his hand and pulled the unfortunate disciple out of the waves and they both returned to the boat. "And when they were come into the ship, the wind ceased. Then they that were in the ship came and worshipped him, saying, Of a truth thou art the Son of God" (Matt. 14:32,33). Judas saw all this with admirable clarity.

Then Judas remembered the words of Jesus spoken in the synagogue of Capernaum, words which caused the greatest part of his disciples to leave Him. It seemed to Judas that he once again heard the Master ask, "Will ye also go away?" (John 6:67). Why did Judas not do as they did? Why did the brusque answer of Simon Peter keep him attached to the Master who had deceived his hopes for a whole year? Why did he not seize the favourable opportunity which Jesus wanted to offer him by saying these words which contrast so strikingly with Peter's declaration, "Have not I chosen you twelve, and one of you is a devil?" (John 6:70). Why did he still remain? Why did the words which Christ had just uttered in the guest chamber make his disciple sink to the depths of such painful memories? Why do we not hear his voice any more? Why is there this moment of oppressive silence? Truly the words of Jesus are incomprehensible if one does not suppose an interruption between "I know whom I have chosen" and "but that the scriptures may be fulfilled." There must have been a silence with a whispered word which cannot have been understood but by one alone, an allusion to a previous declaration which must have produced deep emotion in the soul of one of the listeners, but only in one. These whispered words are those which we mentioned just now, "And one of you is a devil." What thoughtfulness this attitude reveals and what a damning light it throws on the somber character of Judas!

Being susceptible, suspicious, and deceitful, Judas transformed all these appeals into so many ways of perdition. This solicitude was regarded by him as so many proofs that the Master was ignorant of the guilty person. Judas wished to betray Christ. He did not wish to betray himself. But all the same how potent in the Bible is this saying uttered by Jesus, "He that eateth bread with me hath lifted up his heel against me" (John 13:18). To understand well the meaning of these words, as Judas understood them, it is expedient to be reminded of two things which these words immediately awakened in the thought of the traitor, and which have lost their significance for us. In the East the fact of eating together renders the guests inviolable. The same dishes become integral parts of their bodies. In a way it would therefore be like fighting against a part of oneself to fight against a man with whom one had had a meal. In the eyes of an oriental only one crime surpassed in horror a lack of compliance with this age-long tradition. That was to render oneself guilty by violating the rights of hospitality in plotting against the host of whole bread he had partaken. And it was this last crime that Judas was going to commit, which he had virtually already committed, since he was only seeking for a favourable opportunity to betray Jesus Christ. That was the first warning Jesus gave him when he made this statement. And this was the second. This crime had already been committed. In the history of Israel, there had been a man base enough to lift his heel against the man whose bread he had eaten — Ahithophel the Gilonite, one of David's counsellors (II Sam. 15-17). And it was to him that Judas and the Jews of his time believed that the Psalmist alluded in the passage cited by Jesus. What a mournful prophecy! And what a relentless light it throws upon the tragic end of Judas! The traitor cannot have been aware of it, one might say. But, what, then, is meant by the declaration which immediately follows it, "Now I tell you before it come, that, when it is come to pass, ye may believe that I am he"? (John 13:19).

Our familiarity with the last talks of Christ and his apostles veils the brilliancy of this relentless light, but the prophecy had its full significance for Judas. It was luminous for him. The somber vision of Ahithophel who ended his days by strangling himself comes before his mind with all the clearness and sobriety of the sacred Scriptures. And yet he still tried to pull himself together. Would it be possible for him to take his own life? Among the Jews suicide was so rare that he could very well have listened to Christ's warning with an unbelieving ear. He had taken his precautions and his plan had been fully calculated. He did not believe himself capable of committing such a folly. After having visualized the picture that Christ had mentally brought before his eyes, he judged himself to be infinitely superior to Ahithophel, who is vexed when he sees that his advice has not been followed because he is accustomed that his opinions should be regarded as coming from God himself so "he saddled his ass and arose and got him home to his house, to his city and put his household in order and hanged himself and died." A more minute examination would have shown Judas a striking analogy between the two situations: Ahithophel had betrayed David; Judas was betraying the Son of Man; Ahithophel leaves Jerusalem because he feels vexed that his advice is not taken. Judas, several days before, had gone to Jerusalem to barter the life of his Master because he had reproved him for his selfish remark. And was there not a third analogy which our Lord mentioned? He could not believe it and the words of Christ finally left his heart incredulous.

But Jesus reading the thoughts of Judas after having said, "Now I tell you before it come," terminates with these words, "that when it is come to pass ye may believe that I am he." The Master was speaking to his disciples about faith, and yet Judas continued to foster incredulous thoughts in his heart. These words, moreover, did not only remind him that the Master was able to read the hearts of his followers, but especially the words "I am" coupled with the verb "to believe" made him hear again the assertion that Christ made to the Jews, "If ye believe not that I am he, ye shall die in your sins" (John 8:24). Everything speaks of death, suicide and sin! The declarations of Christ to his disciples which at first sight appear to have no relation to one another, on the contrary converge towards the same purpose with marvellous logic. They are all destined to awaken remorse, being rapidly spoken one after another. They are, however, bound together by a tie which escapes the inattentive listener, though Judas whose faculties were at high tension at this moment knows very well. They came like waves gradually lapping higher and higher beating again and again against the rock of resistance. What a sight, both tragic and sorrowful, to see Christ sacrifice some of the last moments which he was spending with his disciples to save a traitor. And then because the traitor resists, even before making a complete revelation, Jesus adds to all the others another useful warning and precedes it with these solemn words, "Verily, verily, I say unto you," of which we have now studied the deep meaning.

"He that receiveth whomsoever I send, receiveth me; and he that receiveth me, receiveth him that sent me" (John 13:20). Thus he brings back to mind his previous declarations about the union of his faithful followers with himself, and his union with God, and the terrible responsibility of the villages which would not receive those he had sent. According to the commandment of his Master, Judas had, in years gone by, shaken the dust of those villages off his feet. He knew that Sodom and Gomorrah would be less severely treated at the day of judgment than those villages: "He that heareth you, heareth me; and he that despiseth you, despiseth me; and he that despiseth me, despiseth him that sent me" (Luke 10:16). This punishment is held over the head of Jesus, but even now our Lord does not pronounce it and is content to recall the warning which accompanied these words, without any apparent relation with those that precede them, warnings which ought, through the memories they awakened, to have touched Judas and made him decide to retrace his footsteps.

If up till then, in his infinite compassion, Christ did not clearly reveal that he was aware of the seriousness of Judas' crime, he knew now that the moment had come not to address the lost sheep indirectly any more. The Good Shepherd was going to call him by name. Since the discretion with which his love had treated him till now had not attained its purpose, He is going little by little to illuminate that lost sheep with all the splendor of his divinity. John in his Gospel marks very clearly the transition from one method to the other. After having pronounced the words which, as we have just seen, should have awakened many memories in Judas, he continues, "When Jesus had thus said, he was troubled in spirit and testified and said . . . . " (John 13:21). The term in our translation rendered by "troubled in spirit" is very powerful. It implies among others the idea of being thoroughly upset, confused and frightened; and when the evangelist even adds that it was in his spirit that Jesus felt troubled, we can believe that at least two of his disciples felt the result — he who alone has chronicled this fact for us because he was leaning his head on Jesus' bosom and he who was on Jesus' other side. Now, we have seen that this man was Judas. Therefore, before even hearing the words which were to act so powerfully on all, Judas felt him tremble when he was going to utter them. This gives stronger power to the solemn introduction, "Verily, verily, I say unto you." And besides that, for the first time, Judas hears an echo of his own words to the chief priests, "I will deliver him unto you." "One of you shall betray me," declared the Master with absolute certitude which John has rendered by "and testified."

Judas had not trembled at the sound of his own voice. But when the echo reverberated in his ears, when someone else pronounced tremblingly the ignoble word of treason, did he not feel horrified, especially when he saw the effect that the revelation of Jesus produced on the eleven? Fear, stupor and consternation was written on all their faces. They looked at one another to know of whom it was that Jesus spake. We have here an indirect proof of the traitor's duplicity, hypocrisy and dissimulation. In their anguish all turn to Christ and ask, "Lord, is it I?" and this question proves how violent the shock had been, because all of them, even Peter, who had just a little while before been so prompt to exculpate himself, recoiled in horror at the idea of such a monstrous act. Everyone, instead of proclaiming his innocence as he would have done in other circumstances in which his innermost being would not have been so deeply stirred, asks with consternation, if he is destined to commit such a crime. This uncertainty weighs so heavily upon them they they are not able to bear it any longer and with one accord all cry, "Lord, is it I?" (Matt. 26:22).

Only one keeps silent. He also is perplexed and troubled, but his trouble is of quite another nature than that of the eleven. Surprised by this sudden outburst which is incomprehensible to him, because he knows very well that none of those who have asked that question will commit the crime, he wonders if his silence has not betrayed him. As they have all expressed their surprise, should he not also have expressed his? And as the others had also done, he looks questioningly at the guests, but with very different intentions. They looked, John tells us, because they knew not of whom he spake; Judas looked to see if his silence had been noticed or if suspicion were visible on the faces of the disciples. No, he sees them lean towards their Master anxiously and await His answer.

Jesus does not appear to have heard this question, or at least he answers it evasively, "He that dippeth his hand with me in the dish, the same shall betray me" (Matt. 26:23). To understand these words properly it is not necessary to suppose that just at that moment Judas, according to Eastern custom, stretched his hand towards the dish. This expression recalls that which Jesus used when molding his thought in accordance with the episode in the Old Testament, "He that eateth bread with me." Understood thus, the words of Christ had a double purpose: to leave the possibility of a doubt so as to allow Judas to repent even now; and also to bring the melancholy catastrophe of Ahithophel before the mind of the traitor who was already feeling a little shaken at the word of treason with which Jesus had characterized his crime.

But he who had persuaded Judas to betray his Master was at work smothering the repentance which would have snatched that soul from his domination. "Far be it from you," the enemy suggested, "to imagine that the fate of Ahithophel should be reserved for you. Because it is necessary, according to the teaching of Jesus himself, that the gospel should be fulfilled, you

are not guilty in effecting its accomplishment." These
words seem to us so subtle that they appear to be little
fitted to convince the unhappy man to whom they were
addressed. Alas! it is always thus with all the temptations that the enemy of souls holds up before our
eyes: they have no power beyond that which they
draw from our hearts. Were such temptations addressed
to others, we should immediately see through such
sophisms or untruths.

How do we know in an absolutely certain way that
it really was thus? The Gospels neither tell us any-
thing about the thoughts of Judas in these circumstances, nor reveal to us the impression produced on
him until the declarations of Jesus. But in transmit-
ting to us the words of our Lord it allows us to
deduce the traitor's state of mind, because Christ read
his heart and his words were an answer to what was
being plotted there. "The Son of man goeth as it
is written of him; but woe unto that man by whom
the Son of man is betrayed! it had been good for that
man if he had not been born" (Mark 14:21). And
note that this declaration, without apparent relation
with that which precedes it, is only comprehensible if
its purpose is either to show Judas once more that his
most secret thoughts do not escape Him who truly
partakes of the prerogatives of the Eternal; or on the
other hand if Christ means to remind him of the truth
which is so often affirmed by the Old Testament, that
all prophecy is conditional of either good or evil. Its
accomplishment depends on the moral attitude that
the individual or the nation thus warned takes in
regard to it. If in face of the punishments which are

prophesied to follow such wickedness, one hardens his
heart and despises the advice of God, then, infallibly,
punishment will be meted out to him. But if on the
contrary he repents, becomes converted and implores
his pardon, he will find a merciful God, slow to anger
and abundant in grace, who will wipe out all his
iniquities. Judas knew this for one cannot suppose
that he lived three years with Jesus without knowing
these prophecies, even if one admits that he had
previously ignored them. His sense of reasoning was
there to tell him that he was lulling himself to sleep
with false illusions in imagining that because his crime
was foretold, it freed him from responsibility in accomplishing it. In spite of this, Christ with His persist-
ent love, adds His own verdict by saying, "But woe
unto that man by whom the Son of man is betrayed."

There is, in these chosen terms, an insistence which
was meant to remind the traitor of the danger into
which he was rushing and make him recoil from the
crime that he was about to commit. How does Christ
describe himself here? He does not say, *"I* go as it is
written of me, but woe unto that man by whom *I* am
betrayed," but, and I ask you to weigh this difference
well, *"The Son of man* goeth as it is written of him,
but woe unto that man by whom the *Son of man*
is betrayed." The Son of man! Those Christians who
only see Christ make an allusion thereby to his human
nature in contrast to his divine nature cannot understand the deep tragedy of these words. Judas knew. He
realized it to the full. This was not a prophet whom he
was on the verge of betraying. This was not even the
Messiah which he and his disciples had expected. It

was the One whom in a vision Daniel saw coming with
clouds of heaven to take possession of the Eternal Kingdom, to execute judgment. It was He who shall be
ashamed before God of those who had been ashamed of
Him and His words. This title used by Jesus hardly veils
his deity. And twice this title reaches in the ears
of him who knew all its significance. The crime that
Judas is planning to commit is the betrayal of God.
When, therefore face to face with the terrible responsibility which He sees him about to take, Christ
pronounces this warning to serve as a mirror in which
he may contemplate his crime with horror, He hopes
that in the presence of the horrible image thus por-
trayed the traitor of God will recoil horrified.

Would Christ have spoken thus if all his efforts were
doomed to failure beforehand, because what is foretold must inevitably happen?

But while the Master is speaking, his disciple continues to be absorbed in quite different thoughts. What
troubles him is the contrast between the anguished
question of all the others and his own silence, especially because of the conclusions that Jesus and
his companions could gather from it. That is why in
answer to his solemn warning the Master hears suddenly, "Lord, is it I?" (Matt. 26:25). Judas wanted to
show that he shared the concern of the others by
asking the same question and yet what a difference
between the two inquiries. While all call Christ "Master" with respectful tenderness Judas uses the officially
cold title of "Rabbi."

Jesus in a voice that we feel broken with emotion
answers, but in such a way that Judas alone can hear

him, "Thou hast said." Can you conceive that if this
revelation had resounded in the guest chamber Peter
would have beckoned to John that he should ask
who it should be of whom he spake? These few words
bring to Judas for the first time the certainty that
Christ knew which of his disciples had sold himself
to Satan in selling Him! Until then, stifling all the dic-
tates of his conscience, he could have imagined that
if the Master had known which one was going to betray him he would not have treated him so long with
such consideration. This argument is impossible now
and the revelation which these words bring to him,
"Thou hast said, " is all the more striking because his
efforts had been so strenuous to cloak the truth. Everything contributed to accentuate this impression: the
tone of Christ's voice and the care which He still took
at this extremity not to betray the traitor. What a
light this merciful attitude throws on Jesus' whole
demeanor during the meal! Thus Judas must have
said to himself, "Although Jesus knew what my plans
were, he had such patience with me, such love and
such compassion, and all that I took for partial ignorance!" What was he to do?

While Judas was silently asking himself that question, Peter beckoned to John that he should ask who
it should be of whom he spake. John was leaning on
Jesus' bosom when Judas asked, "Lord, is it I?" We
have here an irrefutable proof of the care that Jesus
took to be heard by Judas alone. Otherwise John who
was sitting next to our Lord would have known who
the traitor was and have pointed him out to Simon
Peter instead of asking Jesus this question.

But what were the means which Jesus used to point
out the traitor to John, and to him alone, according
to his own testimony when he asserts that when Judas
went out none of those who were at table understood why Jesus said to him, "That thou doest, do
quickly"? This ignorance would be incomprehensible
if one does not admit that everything precedent was
pronounced in an undertone and that our Lord was
able to give Judas the sop without attracting the
attention of the other disciples. But, this was not possible except in two cases: that either Judas was leaning
his head on Jesus' breast, and we know that that place
was occupied by John, or else Jesus himself bent his
head towards the traitor. It is to this conclusion that
we must come. It accounts for Jesus' answer to John,
"He it is to whom I shall give a sop, when I have dipped
it" (John 13:26). It is an appeal, and adoration
hesitates between the solemnity of the warning, the
delicacy of the designation, and the unfathomable
love which prompted both. Do we not feel a thrill
surge through our veins? If we did not know how this
struggle was going to end, would we not intuitively
feel that we were approaching the denouément and
that the son of perdition was going to be thrown into
the depths of hell forever unless he was touched by
so much love and became converted at the last hour?

But powerful though our impression may be, more
powerful still was the impression that Judas felt, because certain peculiarities of the sign which Jesus used
although they are not always present to our memory
when we read this account, could not have escaped
Judas. During the meal of the passover the father of the

family offered to the guests bread dipped in a stew
of fruit, boiled in wine. Jesus conformed to this custom. That is why he does not say, "He it is, to whom
I shall give a sop when I have dipped it" but *the* sop
which was so traditionally well-known. And besides as
Christ was celebrating the passover with his disciples,
that is, with guests, it was a special honour for Judas
to receive this sop and a supremely delicate appeal
to his conscience. Should he not have understood by
this act that the Good Shepherd was seeking for his
lost sheep and had left in the fold the ninety-nine
others which had no need of repentance? In choosing
this way to point out the traitor, did Jesus not show
that He still considered him as one of his own and
looked upon himself as a physician sent to those who
are ill and not to those who are in good health? The
attitude that Judas could still adopt was to recognize
his guilt and ask for pardon. The resistance, which
he made, ended in surrendering his proud soul to
Satan. John following with anxiety all the movements
of Christ as he alone knew their tragic sense, saw re-
flected on Judas' face, as impenitently he took the
fatal sop, the terrifying horror of what was being
enacted in the heart of the traitor, "Satan entered
into him" (John 13:27).

The struggle was finished, at least that part of it
which was enacted in the guest chamber. Still once
more in the Garden of Gethsemane our Lord tried to
bring the lost sheep back to the fold. But, at this time
knowing that, all his efforts would be in vain, He
only adds, "That thou doest, do quickly." The com-
parative degree is really used in the original text

and these few words bring us for a moment at least
a last revelation of our Lord's mercy. John knew the
name of the traitor. He was going to tell Peter. Hasty,
passionate and impulsive as he was, would he not
grasp his sword and throw himself on him who for
so long had abused his Master's confidence? Jesus
would have been able to save Judas from the fate that
he deserved. But what confusion in this quiet meeting!
The other apostles would quickly learn the cause of
this sudden burst of anger and the last talk which
Jesus had with his loved ones and the last instructions
He wished to give them would have been disturbed
by the remembrance of this scene. Was it not to prevent all this and save Judas from being punished for
his great crime before his appointed hour that Christ
allowed no delay?

John terminates his account with these words which
are tragic in their conciseness, "And it was night"
(John 13:30). The thrill which surges through us
in hearing them repeated in our own language is
nothing in comparison with what the first readers of
the gospel felt and those who have the primitive text
before them still today. In the original Greek seven
letters sufficed for the apostle to give an impression
of terror which takes hold of us at the end of his
story. The Greek expression recalls hurried flights
through the darkness, unreasoning panics, phantoms
which peopled the mysterious twilight hours, wild
beasts which roam about seeking for prey, thieves who
enter to steal, and men brutalized by drink. A feeling
of fear, cold, uncertainty, and sin rises within us at
this expression! Through the streets of Jerusalem, the

fateful man proceeds, startled at every instant by the slightest noise that breaks the silence. He was going to the chief priests to fulfill his promise because the suitable moment had come: it was night.

There are, especially in the East, beautiful nights when the brilliant stars shine in an almost inky black sky, or where the moon casts a soft light over everything and makes the world look as if it had been lit up from underneath. But that night was not beautiful. It was cold, for in the courtyard of the chief priest a fire had been lit. It was dark, for soldiers armed with swords and sticks lighted themselves with torches. Darkness reigned supreme. Everything was in darkness around the man who crept along the walls and walked quickly as if pursued by invisible enemies. And within himself was greater darkness still.

Did the man, who went along taking advantage of the night in order to betray Christ to His enemies, give a thought to those other nights his Master had spent in prayer? No, he fled from these thoughts. He fled from the guest chamber. He fled from the look full of love and reproach which was cast upon him; he fled to obey the Master's injunction, "That thou doest, do quickly."

How was it that the tone of his voice, the darkness that surrounded him and the errand which he was proceeding did not bring back to his memory the words which the Master pronounced before accomplishing the two miracles which most excited the rage of his enemies: the healing of the man blind from his birth and the resurrection of Lazarus. "I must work the works of him that sent me, while it is day; the

night cometh when no man can work" (John 9:4).
And what a difference between these works and the
works of Judas, between Him who had sent Christ
and him whose sinister messenger Judas was! "Are
there not twelve hours in the day? If any man walk
in the day he stumbleth not because he seeth the light
of this world. But if a man walk in the night he
stumbleth because there is no light in him" (John 11:
9, 10). Was Judas not having the practical experience
of this truth?

But Judas continued to advance, determined not
to listen because he had refused to obey the orders
of our Lord, "Walk while ye have the light, lest
darkness come upon you: for he that walketh in darkness knoweth not whither he goeth" (John 12:35).
He imagined that he was giving the formal lie to
the words of the Master. He believed that he knew
toward what he was hastening — first of all to the
palace of the chief priests and then to the Garden of
Gethsemane with the soldiers placed under his orders,
and afterwards . . . Afterwards! Having accomplished
his betrayal, did he imagine that he would enjoy the
peace of his crime? The mad man! He was swiftly
approaching the hour when he would be overwhelmed
by despair and would put an end to his days!

During three years this man had been the companion
of Him who could say, "I am the light of the world,"
and because he had refused to be enlightened by it
he had gradually been overcome by darkness. Now the
last rays of the light had expired and darkness reigned
in the heart of Judas, for the Prince of this world had
driven out the King of Glory. Darkness had taken

the place of the Sun of Justice. And it was night! What a tragic ending to the most tragic of stories!

Part Three

"Judas, betrayest thou the Son of man with a kiss?" — LUKE 22:48

Part Three

After having shown how Judas scorned all the appeals of his Master, we finished the preceding study with the mournful words, "And it was night." Let us now resume the sequence of events. Judas went in great haste to the palace of the chief priests. There he obtained a troop of soldiers armed with swords and staves. And because this offence required capital punishment, and the chief priest had the intention of accusing Jesus of being an enemy of Caesar, the Roman cohort had to take part in the arrest. He then insisted that they should go to the tower Antonia and that the Roman soldiers should join the band of armed men and officers which the chief priests and Pharisees had put at his disposal. And when everything was ready he went to the Garden of Gethsemane, knowing that Jesus ofttimes resorted thither with his disciples.

We find here the first indication of a mixture of prudence, which leaves nothing to chance, in combining everything for the success of the odious plot; and an almost feverish haste, for two hours had hardly expired since Judas left the guest chamber. Although he was betraying his Master and just because he was betraying Him, he was seized with terror at the thought that, as so many other times, this holy victim might

escape those who wished to seize Him. Had he not
been a witness to the crowd, who, exasperated by the
two examples of Elijah and Elisha that Jesus had given
them, rose up and thrust Him out of the city and led
him unto the brow of the hill whereon their city was
built? But He passing through the midst of them went
his way (Luke 4:25-30). The chief priests without
doubt had told him the answer of the officers that
were sent to capture the prophet on the last day, that
great day of the feast, "Never man spake like this man"
(John 7:46), and he knew how Jesus had there again
evaded his enemies. He recalled how the people, scan-
dalized by the solemn declaration, "Verily, verily, I say
unto you, Before Abraham was, I am," had taken up
stones to cast at him; but Jesus hid himself and went
out of the temple (John 8:58,59). In the same way
Jesus escaped the multitude in Jerusalem at the feast
of the dedication where they tried to lay hands on Him
(John 10:39). Finally in the beginning of the week,
on the day that he entered Jerusalem, Christ hid himself once more from them (John 12:36).

The thought of all the manifestations of the power
of his Master could not hold back the unhappy man.
On the contrary he was stimulated in his impious
zeal, and it was just these manifestations which urged
him to leave nothing to chance and thus prevent another disappearance. He knew how to maneuver things
so well with the Gentile authorities that the tribune
himself was to command his men. These legionaries
knew no fear. They would not retreat like the Jews
and the presence of their captain would maintain dis-
cipline if a panic were to break out. So the demon

which possessed him left him enough reasoning power to provide all these precautions, yet not enough for him to understand the vanity of such measures after all he had witnessed. If Christ had willed otherwise, what could people armed with swords and sticks, or even Roman soldiers have done? Of what use would lights and torches have been had He willed to flee?

Once having gathered his followers together, Judas was still obsessed by the desire to prevent confusion in the fever of arrest or the voluntary substitution of one of the disciples ready to sacrifice himself for his Master. Desirous also probably to play the first role in the horrible scene, which he foresees without compromising himself with Jesus, he gave them this signal, "Whomsoever I shall kiss, that same is he" (Matt. 26: 48). And still haunted with the same fear, he gave them this order which might appear superfluous addressed to such people, "hold him fast." Is not this haste in the execution of his plot and the rapidity with which he led the troops to the Garden of Gethsemane a proof in itself of his constant uneasiness? Christ should not be given time to escape. He had calculated everything so well in advance and prepared his plot so well, as we have seen, two hours had sufficed for the traitor to go from the guest chamber to the palace of the high priest to arrange everything and thence proceed to the other side of the Kedron.

Before crossing the brook with the traitor, let us consider for a moment the real reason for this haste. Judas imagined that he knew the reason, for he believed, as we have just shown, that to act quickly was the only way of acting surely. He did not see that in this point he was unconsciously following the advice given to Absalom by Ahithophel which sad example our Lord had called to mind in the guest chamber. He did not know who it was that lashed him to such fevered activity and thus prevented his victim from regaining possession of himself. Satan had entered into him and he did not intend that Judas through any introspection of his own conduct or a moment's reflection should be able to repent until it was too late. He determined to create an irreparable breach between Jesus and his unhappy disciple. Once the terrible crime was perpetrated and his Master was in the hands of his murderers, the traitor would have to think of the terrible act that he had just committed. There would be time enough for him to surrender to despair, but not enough to feel the effects of repentance and implore pardon.

What a lesson! The voice of God certainly commands us not to harden our hearts on the day that we shall hear the voice of the Lord. But it is nevertheless true that there is a certain agitation which is directly inspired by the Prince of darkness. The activity which he suggests for people is not harmful in itself, but he always arranges things so that his victim will not have the chance of pulling himself together till he has definitely separated him from Jesus Christ. Is this not the reason that the world who is the faithful servant of this prince multiplies distractions of all sorts? It is not necessary that they should even be dangerous by what they evoke. They may in themselves be quite reasonable and even legitimate. The wrong consists in their multiplicity and the enervation which they provoke. They render it impossible for us to reflect on the real sense of life — the one thing needful when we have to appear before omnipotent God. But if this is true of the occupations which become dangerous simply because they are an obstacle to meditation, what must we think of the activity which took possession of Judas and which the devil lashed into insatiability?

Everything was conducive to serious reflection — if the traitor had been in a fit state to think at all. To make him recoil it would have been enough for him to look at the troop of soldiers which he was leading and to think of the destiny which Jesus had reserved for him and of the role that he was actually playing. The people armed with swords and staves and the Roman soldiers which grouped round them were sworn enemies. That night, as the text tells us, not only did the two parties of the Jewish nation appear to be reconciled but even Jews and Gentiles forgot their race hatred, the oppressed uniting with their oppressors, and the servants of the chief priests marching side by side with the Romans. In the depths of their souls they wished for the destruction of submission of that uncircumcised race. What was the bond that united them? It was the hatred that they all felt against one man because He had unmasked their hypocrisy, and this hatred was so strong that for the moment it dominated that which separated them. He had an influence over the people of which they were jealous. And to make the contrast still more lurid, and to show the incongruous character of these associates, it was a disciple of this man who led them! A disciple permitted the Pharisees, chief priests, and Romans to wreak their vengeance in pointing out Him whose teachings he had studied for three years, whose love had never ceased to surround him, who, even unto the last moment, had done everything to bring him back.

Yes, it was a disciple, one who according to the intention of Christ was to preach the gospel and guide souls to the Saviour. Won by his preaching, Pharisees, Sadducees, and Gentiles would forget their old animosity to form only one community of brotherhood where the name of Christ would be exalted, the teachings of the Messiah serve for rules of conduct, and his transforming love cover all. And behold him here uniting men with such different aspirations and with such tenacious animosity. He inspired them with a single thought and led them, it is true, to Jesus; but only to carry out their criminal intentions and seize Him with violence!

It was by a kiss that Judas proposed to point out the Master to his enemies, and he did not tremble in giving them such a signal! But the feeling of horror which fills us when we hear these words would be much stronger if we could read them in the original text. The connection which we establish between a kiss and affection comes from custom. We could quite easily conceive that it might have been different, and we even know that many peoples do not show their friendship thus. But in Greek to kiss someone or treat him as a friend is the same word. One could therefore translate the words of Judas, "It is he that I shall kiss" or "him to whom I shall show affection." And he did not feel in pronouncing these words what another infamous thing he had added to his act of treason. He chose a sign of affection and even of great tenderness to betray our Lord!

But Judas did not stop there. Although he was enticed by him who dominated him not to yield to any halfway measures, yet he strove to keep up a correct attitude towards his fellow disciples. Though troops surrounded him he did not feel absolutely safe, for he knew that they had swords. He knew how passionate Peter was and did not wish to run the risk of being his victim while all attention would be concentrated on Christ to whom they must "do violence," according to the powerful expression in the original text. He intended to make it appear as if he had come by chance into the Garden of Gethsemane with the troop of soldiers that he was leading. He knew the other apostles well enough to hope that they had not understood the brief dialogue between himself and Jesus Christ, and that they had not seized the meaning of the sop and the reason for his hasty flight. And we know, according to John (John 13:28) that in this supposition he was not mistaken. Did he hope to divert Jesus Christ's intention through artful means? It is possible that the lack of conscience inspired by Satan should even lead him to this depth. So Judas proceeded to the retreat where Jesus had chosen to spend in prayer the last moments of liberty that he would have on earth before his crucifixion. The life of the traitor was drawing to its end. The last chance of repentance was now being offered to him.

But why does John begin his account of these decisive events with these words, "When Jesus had spoken these words he went forth with his disciples over the brook Kedron, where was a garden into the which he entered, and his disciples. And Judas also which betrayed him, knew the place: for Jesus ofttimes resorted thither with his disciples"? (John 18:1,2). Why do the other three apostles, though with some difference in detail, specially mention with significant agreement that Jesus went to the Mount of Olives? (Matt. 26:30; Mark 14:26; Luke 22:39). Was it only to show that notwithstanding all appearances and the powers in league against him Jesus could have escaped from their clutches had he so desired, as he had so often done before his hour had come, in support of the truth proclaimed by Christ himself, "I lay down my life that I might take it up again. No man taketh it from me, but I lay it down of myself. I have power to lay it down, and I have power to take it again"? (John 10: 17,18). This declaration is evident from the words of the text. The evangelists wish to draw our attention to another truth. If we remember the efforts of Jesus to warn Judas in the guest chamber and if we read the story of Ahithophel to whom, as we have seen, Christ alluded, we shall understand this insistence in mentioning the Kedron and the Mount of Olives. Through the choice that our Master made of the place of his arrest, we see another attempt to pull his misguided apostle back from the abyss.

The Kedron! It was after David had passed over this torrent that he said to Zadok, "Carry back the ark of God into the city" (Jerusalem) (II Sam. 15:23,25). And the Mount of Olives! It was while David went up the Mount of Olives that one came to tell him, saying, "Ahithophel is among the conspirators with

Absalom," and that the king cried, "O Lord, I pray thee, turn the counsel of Ahithophel into foolishness" (II Sam. 15:30,31). On this hill Judas guessed the place where it came to pass that when David was come to the top of the mount, Hushai the Archite came to meet him, which meeting decided the fate of Ahithophel (II Sam. 15:32).

But these recollections of events in the history of his nation, which were enacted in these very places were not the only recollections. Even more distinctly were the memories associated with the banks of the Kedron and the Mount of Olives where Judas had been with the eleven disciples — and Jesus. What singular virtue places possess where we have conversed with those we love! It is as if every detail of a landscape even unconsciously brings back to us an echo of the conversations that we had in passing there. Jesus wished to make use of this concept to make once more an indirect appeal to Judas. How many times, in reality, during that week did Christ not pass along the way from Bethany to Jerusalem, as the gospel indicates in plain language! On the day of his triumphal entrance when he was come nigh to the Mount of Olives from which the city appeared to the admiration of the pilgrims, in striking contrast with the enthusiasm of the multitude, he wept over it and uttered these strange words, "If thou hadst known, even thou, at least in this thy day, the things which belong unto thy peace! but now they are hid from thine eyes" (Luke 19:41,42). Did a poignant regret not pierce his heart? Did he not understand that for him as well as for the holy city this was an hour of visitation? But these things were hid from his eyes!

These memories were specially pregnant in the garden of Gethsemane, as John draws our attention to the fact that "Judas knew the place: for ofttimes Jesus resorted thither with his disciples." If only we knew the words that passed in the conversation to which the disciple alludes as well as those words addressed by his Master to His disciples in the guest chamber, we could better determine the exact nature of this appeal. And even though we do not know them, we can still gather an idea of the impression that the traitor must have felt entering with the enemies of Christ into this garden he had so often entered with his Master.

It was night! Calmness reigned over the whole country. The hour of intimate conversation had come! One after another of the disciples questioned Jesus about his teachings to the crowd which they had understood imperfectly, and of which they themselves had hardly fathomed the depth. How many times had Judas seen his Master there in prayer! He was passing now near the trees sanctified by such holy memories that each one should have spoken to him. But did you remember, Judas? It was there with a face illumined with an inward flame nad rendered more aglow by communion with his Father that Jesus looked at you. It was there that these words proceeded out of his mouth which were apparently addressed to all but which he meant for you. Yes, it was there! Escaping, however, from all these voices, from the eloquent trees about him, even from his own heart, he went on still trying to pierce the darkness to find the group he was seeking.

Suddenly out of the shadows a man appeared. It was he! On his face were still the traces of a supreme struggle, his brow and his cheeks bore the marks of the drops of blood which, during his agony had fallen down to the ground (Luke 22:44). Judas was ignorant of what had happened, but he saw the face illumined with the celestial beauty which of yore he had seen when Christ had come to his disciples in this very place. He heard a well-known voice ring in his ears, but it was not his past memories which brought the echo back to him. It was the voice of the man who separating himself from his disciples had advanced alone before the troop of soldiers, surrendering himself to the rage of his enemies. The question which he asked them, "Whom see ye?" (John 18:4), might have reminded Judas of the one his Master asked two of his disciples at the beginning of his teaching on the banks of the Jordan. John had often told him about the first meeting with their Master. Then he had said to them, "What seek ye?" (John 1:38), choosing this form for his appeal. Now he said, *"Whom* seek ye?" Judas had not time to indulge in any salutary reflection because the cohort at once cried, "Jesus of Nazareth" (John 18:5). With such calmness that all were terrified and with such majesty that they all went backwards and fell to the ground, Jesus answered in these simple words, "I am he."

It was not the first time that Judas had heard these words. Once during the night on the Lake of Galilee the winds were contrary. On the preceding day Jesus had fed five thousand men with five loaves and two fishes. And then because this multitude wished to carry

him away to make him a king he had fled to a high
mountain to pray. That was why his disciples were
alone in the tempest on the lake (Matt. 14:26). Suddenly they saw a human form coming towards them
walking on the wild waves. In the belief that they had
seen a phantom they cried out with terror. It was
then that they heard his voice say unto them, "It is I,
be not afraid" (John 6:20). In the Garden of Gethsemane these consoling words were omitted because
he who was coming towards them did not present
himself as Saviour coming to the help of his loved
ones, but as Judge who without doubt was going to
pronounce capital sentence against the guilty prostrate
before him. For a second time they heard his voice
asking the same question, "Whom seek ye?" and the
same astonished response from all the soldiers, "Jesus
of Nazareth" (John 18:7). This time Christ answered,
"I have told you that I am he: if therefore ye seek me
let these go their way," pointing with his hand to the
disciples who gathered near to defend him (John 18:8).

Not here, any more than in the guest chamber, did
Judas realize the mercy that this action expressed
towards him. Do we understand it, although we have
so often read the words with which John begins his
account, "Jesus, therefore, knowing all things that
should come upon him"? (John 18:4). Our Lord sur-
rendered to the soldiers to render unnecessary the sign
of most tender affection by which the traitor had intended to point out the Master to his persecutors and
thus violate old established custom, for if the Master
sometimes gave one of his disciples a kiss, a disciple,
on the contrary, never kissed his Master.

Judas was not moved to pity by these considerations. He feared that if he did not give the agreed signal he would lose the profit that he was expecting from this treason, because the tribune knowing his victim now would fulfill his duty and take possession of the defenceless prophet. So he quickly regained his self-assurance, drew near, and kissed Judas several times. I say several times, although the kiss of Judas has become proverbial for the original text tells us with vigorous conciseness that the traitor kissed the face of Christ from top to bottom, after having pronounced these words, "Hail, Rabbi" (Matt. 26:49). And to the double cynicism which the sacred writers have kept intact for us, we may add a third. The customary greeting was "peace be with you" and it is quite probable that Judas used this expression before giving Christ the kisses mentioned by the first two evangelists. How did the man dare to speak of joy and peace since he had enjoyed neither from the day that he sought how he might conveniently betray Jesus to the chief priests? Did he hope to hear the customary answer "peace be with you"? He would have waited in vain. After the departure of the traitor from the guest chamber He who had said to his loved ones, "Peace I leave with you, my peace I give unto you" (John 14:27), could neither leave peace with, nor give it to this fallen being who bowed down before Him.

And still Jesus answered by addressing a last appeal to Judas. There is no doubt that if he had heard it quickly enough Judas would have found therein the means of salvation, but only after much suffering and anguish of sincere repentance. For if he were to brush

aside this warning now he would throw himself into
the slough of despair which leads to madness and
suicide. And with what gentleness did Christ display his
goodness and love and complete self-forgetfulness. But
at the same time there was a warning in this last
appeal of which Matthew and Luke have each transmitted a part to us, so that to have it in its primitive form we must combine the testimony of the two
evangelists, "Friends, wherefore art thou come? Judas,
betrayest thou the Son of man with a kiss" (Matt.
26:50, Luke 22:48). How one feels every word vi-
brating with Christ's emotion at this last effort! He
concentrated therein everything that could touch the
heart and conscience or soul of him who was a disciple and yet was betraying his Master. In these words,
where every word tells, we may sum up all the im-
pressions that we have gathered during these studies.
They are all the more striking, they derive still more
solemnity from the fact that they were the last words
of Jesus which the traitor heard before the final
judgment.

Let us briefly review the different aspects of this
sentence. The Saviour with the solicitude of a father
for his misguided child called Judas by his Christian
name to remind him of the declaration of the gospel,
"I have called thee by thy name, thou art mine"
(Isaiah 43:1) and similarly by the word "friend"
brought back to his memory the hours passed in the
service of his Master. Christ could not have said
"friend" as our versions are translated, because according to His Word, His friends are those who obey His
commandments (John 15:14). "Why are you here?"

literally means, "For what purpose are you here?" Yet our Lord was not ignorant of the motives which brought his disciple to the Garden of Gethsemane, as is proved by what followed. The interrogative form which Jesus used was meant to make Judas examine his own thoughts, consider the motives of his conduct and compare the criminal intentions that he was concealing with the attitude that a disciple should adopt when coming before his Master. That was why our Lord asked, "Betrayest thou the Son of man with a kiss?"

The word on which the accent falls emphasizes best this monstrous dissimulation, for it was destined to move Judas in tearing away the whole disguise of his hypocrisy. To render in our language the effect produced by the original text one should say, "You are betraying the Son of man by a sign of affection." We have just seen what Jesus meant by these words, "Son of man," and added to the others what a solemn warning this expression contained! Then Jesus had addressed Judas indirectly. He could have pretended not to have understood. But now it was expressed in clear language without any possible confusion. Now He no longer said, "Woe unto that man by whom the Son of man is betrayed" (Matt. 26:24) but "Thou betrayest the Son of man." Alas, all this solicitude was in vain. The son of perdition remained deaf, and voluntarily thrust aside this last offer of salvation.

After having seen so far the progressive hardening of this perverse soul, let us now see the sudden awakening which Matthew tells with impressive conciseness, "Then Judas which had betrayed him, when he saw that he was condemned, repented himself, and brought again the thirty pieces of silver to the chief priests and elders, saying, I have sinned in that I have betrayed the innocent blood" (Matt. 27:3,4). How much is contained in these few words! Try to imagine how a writer of romance or an historian would have treated the poignant ending of such a tragic life! How many admirable pages and what exciting developments would they not have accumulated, without succeeding in touching the deepest fibers of our being, as the sacred writer does by the very simplicity of his narrative. In spite of the extreme conciseness everything is told us because every word contains in itself a world of revelation. All the appeals of Christ, as we have seen, were in vain. Even his look was ineffectual, although this same look in the court of the chief priest had stirred Peter so deeply that he went out and wept bitterly (Luke 22:61,62).

But at last the condemnation of Him whom he had just betrayed brought up in Judas' heart the conviction of sin. How can we explain this mystery?

One might be tempted to suppose that in betraying his Master Judas wished to precipitate events and oblige Christ to defend himself, to annihilate his enemies, and thereupon proclaim himself the Messiah that the Jews expected. But then, how can we explain the attitude of Christ towards his disciples or the serious and insistent appeals that he addressed to him in the guest chamber and even in the Garden of Gethsemane? How can we conceive Judas not recognizing his mistake when our Lord himself came before those who were seeking him or when he commanded

Peter, "Put up again thy sword into his place: Thinkest thou that I cannot now pray to my Father, and he shall presently give me more than twelve legions of angels?" (Matt. 26:52,53); or when he turned towards the soldiers, "Are ye come out as against a thief with swords and staves for to take me? I sat daily with you teaching in the temple, and ye laid no hold on me. But all this was done that the scriptures of the prophets might be fulfilled"? (Matt. 26:55,56). Why after such categorical statements did Judas wait for the shattering of his dreams to understand that Christ was not the Messiah that he expected?

We think that there is another explanation of this mystery. The cross of Christ, one has rightly said, is the supreme revelation of sin. And the first person on whom it exercised this influence, even in anticipation, was Judas! "And having bound him, they led him away, and delivered him to Pontius Pilate the governor. Then Judas which had betrayed him, when he saw that he was condemned, repented himself" (Matt. 27:2,3). What feelings are evoked by the simple word "Then"! It was thus that the same evangelist, as we have seen, began his account with the first meeting between the traitor and the chief priests (Matt. 26:14). There Matthew explains the contrast between the words of Jesus "Let her alone," and the action of the disciple.

And here Matthew marks the sudden transition from past conduct to present resolution. Then, when the image of the ignominious death which was awaiting his Master was flashed across his mind by the fact that they were leading the condemned man before Pontius

Pilate, suddenly, but too late, light came to him. He
saw his terrible crime in its right proportions. To some
extent, repentance at last entered the soul that had not
ceased to harden itself. When the crime had been perpetrated and an irreparable breach created between
Jesus and Judas, the Prince of darkness released his
hold for a time.

Yet Satan did not allow his victim to escape com-
pletely. That is why I said that "to some extent repentance entered the soul of Judas." In reality the
word "repentance" has not an exact equivalent in our
language. The word "repent," which certain versions
use is too strong; and "regret," which others have
adopted, is too weak. This is only a shade of difference,
it is true, but in such a tragic episode the most minute
differences indicated by the text to guide us in our
study have their value. Feeling was so strong that it
compelled him to act — "He brought again the thirty
pieces of silver to the chief priests and elders." He
turned aside from the money with horror; for everything in the palace where his Master had just been condemned reminded him of the moment when he had
promised to betray his Master and had received payment for his treason.

Yet the betrayer's words are more remarkable than
his restitution, because in all the New Testament only
one other time do we hear this cry of a soul conscious
of its fault, "I have sinned" (Luke 15:18,21). In the
parable of the prodigal son the absolute identity of the
words raises this question in our mind: In using it
did Judas remember the prodigal son and the pardon
that the Father granted as a symbol of the infinite

love of God for all sinners? One can almost be sure
for it is so rare to hear a man recognize his mistakes
so frankly and categorically, "I have sinned in that I
have betrayed the innocent blood." That is all. Judas
does not try to make Satan responsible for his crime
and yet we know that the devil had put into the
heart of Judas Iscariot the thought to betray Jesus and
had entered into him to strengthen his resolution
(John 13:2,27). He could have mentioned other accomplices still. It is not without reason that the text
renders us attentive to these words, "They delivered
him to Pontius Pilate the governor. Then Judas which
had betrayed him, repented himself." He who was
guilty did not take cover behind the treason of other
accomplices to slink away from the truth which terrified him. He did not say "We have sinned," but "I have
sinned." Neither did he try to extenuate the guilt
of his terrible crime nor reassure himself in reasoning
thus, "The chief priests of the people, the representatives of Jehovah, are the sworn enemies of my Master.
They led him away bound to Pilate the Roman Governor. Therefore he is not the Messiah." He was not
afraid of provoking their anger by his frankness. No
more of his former excuses! Now he did not say, "Jesus
has deceived my Messianic hopes." He recognized and
openly confessed his mistake without troubling to jus-
tify it, "I have sinned in that I have betrayed the innocent blood." And it is a remarkable thing that this
expression is only found here to denote the Master.

Although Judas' repentance was so sincere and his
conversion so touching, this complete confession leaves
indifferent those whom it should have moved. To him

who they abandoned after he had served their iniqui-
tous purpose they were satisfied to give this cold ironi-
cal answer, "What is that to us? see thou to that" (Matt.
27:4). One feels tempted, is it not true, to scourge
such indifference as it deserves? But we are studying
the character of Judas and not the chief priests. So
we must, therefore, consider the consequences of their
attitude on the repentant traitor. They were terrible.
These words drove the sting of responsibility into his
desperate soul. "How could I see to that?" he must have
said to himself, "after having disregarded the Master's
most tender appeals and tried his long-suffering patience in the Garden of Gethsemane, after having
covered his face with hypocritical kisses? How could I
bear life," he must have said to himself, "darkened
with such remembrances? He is going to die! And as
I cannot save him through repentance I will precede
him in death." Then he cast down the pieces of silver
in the temple, and departed and went and hanged
himself.

Thus after having recognized the monstrosity of his
actions, Judas felt such a desire to retrieve his errors
that at any cost he must get rid of the accursed money
which was the price for his treason, and after having
confessed his crime with exemplary sincerity, Judas
nevertheless ends in despair and suicide! He "went and
hanged himself." What failed Judas at this last
hour? Ah! if shaken by scorn of mankind, instead of
sinking into the depths of despair, he had turned his
steps to Calvary, and there, prostrate before the cross,
had repeated the cry that the chief priests had heard,
"I have sinned," he could have obtained the pardon of

Him who opened the gates of paradise for the criminal crucified at His side. Yes, His infinite love would have reached so far. The grace of God is unlimited enough to give us this certainty. But it came too late. The restriction did not come from God. It came from Judas. He did not know, one might say, the declaration, "If we confess our sins God is faithful and just to forgive us our sins." And yet how the whole attitude of his Master towards him corroborated the experience of the Psalmist, "I acknowledged my sins unto thee and mine iniquity have I not hid . . . and thou forgavest the iniquity of my sins" (Ps. 32:5).

What a warning for us and an illustration of his inspired Word. "Today if ye will hear his voice, harden not your hearts."

Let us read once more the ending of this sacred story. "Then Judas which had betrayed him, when he saw that he was condemned, repented himself, and brought again the thirty pieces of silver to the chief priests and elders, saying, 'I have sinned in that I have betrayed the innocent blood.' Then he cast down the pieces of silver in the temple, and departed and went and hanged himself!"